GLUTEN FREE

FREAK

Finding My Way in a World Full of Pasta

By Marianne Meeder

Dedication

This book is dedicated to my dear friend Princess Tereya Grace Philemon whose love and encouragement gave me wings to take flight. For me becoming gluten free is like being born again. It is like I am really living for the very first time. This book is also dedicated to everyone who needs to start their life over and be born again.

Table of Contents

Gluten Free Freak

I never thought I would be one of those people. You know the kind who cringe at the sight of bread, pasta and pastries. Carbs were my friend and gluten my lover. Until one day my lover betrayed me. I never saw it coming. I mean never. I had been on a round of three antibiotics over the course of the past year and just overcame a virus. Or should I say the virus overcame me.

I woke up one day with food allergies, food sensitivities, leaky gut and digestive disorder. I didn't order any of this off the menu. It just served me papers one day and there I was trapped and served a label I never wanted. It completely disrupted my life for months on end, until I figured it out. Paleo, what is that a form of dinosaur?

Paleo became my friend as it meant I could eat another version of sugary stuff and it was better for me like the original caveman and cavewoman I guess. Paleo is purer and simpler in its original raw form. I could choose almond flour, coconut flour, and endless possibilities of flours.

But it was not an easy journey. I lived in denial at first and that is not a river in Egypt. It was a place of unwanted expectation. A place you can't or shouldn't linger for very long. Climb aboard my boat and let's journey together sailing into freedom, access to unlimited power in every area of your life and complete transformation. Life can be good again gluten free, holidays and every day. You have to accept what has been dished up to you on your plate so to speak and create a whole new life map. That is what I learned the hard way. But the life mapping part includes not just what comes off your plate, but everything within your power to add to your plate; the full richness and sweetness you truly deserve.

Whenever I ate my usual friends, brownies and pancakes or cookies they became my mortal enemies inflicting such torture on my gut. Who wants to serve up a heaping spoonful of self-punishment with every meal?

I had never understood it before what gluten can do to a body, until it happened to me. It actually altered my personality. I am a super loving and friendly gal who answers every phone call. I became irritable, cranky, resistant to people and withdrawn. I wasn't even aware of it at first. That is because gluten wreaks havoc in your entire body. It is like the devil incarnate has landed in your joints. Our guts are a powerful force. All my joints swelled up. I couldn't even walk right from the swelling. It is the most miserable thing on the planet to wake up and be living in this gluten nightmare and feeling like a ghost of a person. The real you lost. A zombie shuffling around like the undead.

I don't like to make a fuss about myself. I am tough and I will get through this. Ordering in a restaurant is fun. I ordered a healthy meal and it came to me smothered with two extra-large slices of garlic bread on the top. I am new at this whole thing, but shouldn't bread stay away from my food? I politely say to the waitress, I didn't order this bread. She stares at me blankly not comprehending. Not everybody gets it. They can't. They don't know what it feels like to wake up with a terrorist living in your joints holding your life hostage and for ransom. So I ask her several times apologizing and clarifying that I can't have bread. I have a food allergy. Note to self: I guess I need to announce as I enter the room gluten allergist coming please clear the room and all bread step aside.

A funny thing happened to me when I was eating Chinese food the other day. It is called cross-contamination I think. I didn't know soy sauce had gluten in it. I just ordered meat and veggies but who knows what else was cooked on the grill. Now this girl is in love with Chinese food and it was my staple. Shortly after my joints began to swell up. I am like say what? I go to lay down very discouraged and heartbroken over these new challenges I don't understand. Are you freaking kidding me? This girl who doesn't like to cook is going to need to cook now at home? I have heard of stay at home moms, but stay at home cooks, me never! The price to pay is too high. I lay down in bed hurting, discouraged and disillusioned about what is overcoming my body.

Donuts, cakes, breads, muffins, pizza where are you my long lost friends? Were you really my friend or more of a frenemy? This whole world is full of gluten. It is everywhere I go I could scream! I am living in a gluten nightmare, being chased by a demon, but it is inside my belly torturing my gut. Get it out of here now!

Growing up I am afraid I was not a nutritional queen. I didn't eat the four food groups. Sure I ate and there were groups: Ding Dongs, Ho Hos, Zingers and Suzy Q's. Those four made a group my dad thought was important. You can't blame him as a single parent he just wanted a kid to have a happy tummy in the moment. Oh for the moments to redeem a life. No wonder my tummy turned freaky. It is payback time.

One of the lessons I never learned is called meal prep. This rat race 21st jungle we live in has got me racing from one thing to the next. I am a grab me and go kind of gal. I go to the grocery store and forget half the things on my list. What list? Let's be honest, I don't shop from a list. Sometimes I don't even shop, I order out. Chinese and pizza were my favs. Kiss that goodbye gluten lover. It must be time for me to change all my evil ways. But how do I do it at this late stage of the game?

Well pain is a big motivator. Also, the fact I love to eat. Nothing motivates one like a love of food. Why aren't there more gluten free restaurants yet? I don't even know of one at this point.

I discovered buckwheat pancakes. I guess buckwheat is not a wheat. Say what? This gluten free world is confusing. But I sure do love my pancakes and miss the wheat taste. Buckwheat is an adjustment. Slap some raspberries and butter along with some good old maple syrup on there. What is so hard is the adjustment to this new world. My taste buds crave sugar and the same old. My soul is craving a makeover. Not just a gluten makeover, but a whole life makeover. This didn't just happen to me, it happened for a reason!

I also discovered since I can't have pasta I found a new LOVE-- ZOODLES. They are all the rage. Zucchini noodles with pesto, olive oil and tomatoes. So amazing! My grocery store even has zoodles fresh daily already zoodled up. I am gradually changing a lifetime of bad habits.

I now take digestive enzymes with every meal to support my digestion. I increased my consumption of bone broth soup as I learn it is good for healing the digestive system and the lining of the gut. The collagen in the bone broth is the health culprit we need. I go to a local butcher and get mine fresh, but there are so many options. I love the idea of the freshest pure source. If I am going clean, I might as well go for broke and get the best benefits.

The Week from Hell

"If your going through hell, keep going."

Winston Churchill

I am newly gluten free, still in denial and not getting it. I go to work parties and impulsively put chocolate chip cookies in my mouth. I just did it shoved about 4 or 5. Don't judge, the title of this book is freak. They were small anyway. My whole life hasn't gotten on board with these necessary changes I have to make. Not a good choice I know. The next day I can barely walk. So now I get it. The failure formula- gluten equals joint pain, emotional pain and the whole nine yards. Tell me you haven't done it at least once, made a choice that was the opposite of the choice you really needed to make? Why can't I HAVE ALL THOSE CHOCOLATE CHIP COOKIES MADE BY THIS NICE MAN'S WIFE? It is really not fair at all. It's a party, a celebration of life here, and the food equals love, comfort, connection to it all. Except my gut won't participate in this party.

Well, let's live and learn. Some of us are slow learners when it comes to change. You'll have to forgive me. I go to a get together with ladies and what gets put in front of me but a plate of decadent brownies with creamy white icing. Just about my all-time fav dessert on God's planet Earth. They are bite size so it doesn't count right? Guess again. For the gluten intolerant all it takes is one bite. Don't even think about it. Don't even put that thing in your mouth. Do you hear me? Guess what happened after I ate it? Well once you head down the road of self-destruction you might as well not turn back. I put a few more in my mouth. Well there is always a price to pay for sin. I woke up with pain in my joints. The devil incarnate got into my joints and is having a party there. But I invited him in, so it's my fault. Time to cast the demon out.

I am stuffing my pain, in denial about what is happening to me. There is a disconnect between my brain and my mouth, between my desire to do the right thing and move on. I don't have time for a pity party about my life because I can't have what everyone else is having on their plate. I can't just get over this lickety split here. Will I never be able to go on a date and have pasta? I don't have time to buy gluten free flours and make gluten free recipes. But baby I haven't got time for the pain! Carly Simon was so right. That is the bottom line. The pain is robbing my life of all the really, good abundance I deserve. So chasing pain is not my answer.

My usual remedy of cover up won't work. I need deliverance; like full blown Exorcism here. The demon is gluten and my ties to loving her. It is hard to break a soul tie. Well this girl is going to have to spin her head around and get it together. I will have to figure out the disconnect from my mouth to my behavior and vice versa. There is a big life out there I dreamed of living and I can't let this shallow love affair ruin it for my true love of life. The apostle Paul himself said, "Sometimes I do the very thing I hate..." He was pretty much a saint who called himself the chief of sinners just like me.

Waking up the next morning after the affair and not feeling so great. I am not talking about sex here but I got your attention. The affair is one in question. The mingling of two souls not meant for each other; gluten and me. You wake up with indigestion, brain fog, mixed with shame and confusion. The best thing to do the day after a gluten indulgence is to be gentle with yourself physically and emotionally. Don't beat yourself up, that has already happened in your gut. DETOX. I think gentle fasting lets the stomach lining recuperate. Drink bone broth soup if you can. To be honest I lay down and am depressed, tired and sad this is happening to me. A feeling of helplessness washing over my soul. But I am in the adjustment phase. I will pass through this phase once I am ready to move forward and once I get the impact here. I am now gluten intolerant and eating ANY of it is not an option for me.

Holy Holidays

"The holidays are only holy if we make them so."

Marianne Williamson

Christmas, New Years, Thanksgiving and more. My delight is over the holidays. What makes them holy to me is the specialness of time with our family and the reason behind each day. But let's not forget the food, oh the glorious wonderful food! It's really all about the food! I am being facetious but really at the heart of the holidays is always the table we feast from laid out with creamy, dreamy, delectable dishes galore.

I accidentally ate cheesy potatoes at Christmas. Well I didn't put two and two together that they put flour in there. I never make cheesy potatoes, how would I know? The next day I wake up and gained 3 lbs. and hurt. This time I decided to try something healing for myself. There is a new acupuncture place offering a free 30 min session. I have nothing to lose. It is called Modern Day Acupuncture. I head out and go for it not expecting much. What I got is a breakthrough. The swelling cleared up and my digestion settled down. I could walk easier and the inflammation subsided. I love acupuncture!

I guess the holidays require more thought. I need to bring a gluten free dish along with me. So many party dishes are all dressed up with gravy and sauce. No gluten free desserts, so I am feeling sad about it all. Fast forward and I discover a gluten free bakery that makes amazing cupcakes with brown rice flour. Next year I will have to plan ahead for the holidays and bring some along. Nobody likes deprivation at the holidays or a lack of choices.

For Thanksgiving I was feeling stressed out going to experience my first gluten free turkey dinner. I almost couldn't stomach it, no pun intended. I made a declaration over my life. This day God is delivering me of my sugar addiction. I am not waiting till the holidays are over and using them as an excuse. I did it! I experienced exactly what I spoke out loud! Total freedom and no sweets! I lost the connection to the food and gained the connection to my family. I put turkey, greens and cranberries on my plate. That was about all. I had an amazing conversation with a friend I don't think I would have had if I was just focused on the food. Giving up something always makes you more present to something else. My greatest breakthrough. God came through in my declaration!

The holidays just keep rolling along and the food is always piling up along with it! A fancy restaurant with the family on New Year's Eve. Let's hear it for the restaurants who put a GF on the menus. This makes life so easy. I am at Ditka's in Chicago. Everybody is ordering up an appetizer and I am wondering which ones have traces of arsenic and lace, AKA flour. That's a throwback to an old Cary Grant movie where they poisoned somebody.

Gluten does the same to those of us intolerant. Well you just gotta roll with it, having time with this amazing family around a gorgeous table of gourmet food is priceless. I could have cancer or be dead or in the hospital. But I get to be here with all of them. So rich, so full is my plate. I know a lot of people who never get along with their family, never see their family even. So I am not going to cry about my food I can't have tonight. It's a new day, a new year in fact. My family is the best so much fun, so much zeal for life. Zest for the incredible. It doesn't matter that I can't eat the same appetizer.

I use my quick GF guide on the menu to spy out my choices. Ahh a gluten free Kale Caesar Salad with no croutons. Those are so yummy. No sense spoiling the New Year, the buzz, the sparkle of it all over what I can't have. I feast on what I can have. I ordered salmon and sweet potatoes. My fav! When dessert came there were no gluten free options. I am actually pretty full. The fun is watching everyone indulge in theirs. You know when did life become all about the food anyway? I am so blessed to be with my family. That makes my plate truly full.

I went to the gym every day and watched my family enjoy lots of amazing Italian homemade decadent cookies. I used to pig out on these as well. No use crying over spilt milk. What can you do? To my delight when I left the house after New Year's I lost 3 pounds. Ahh good things come to those committed. Coming home from the holidays I slept like a baby cause my stomach was a lot lighter. Our lives are full when we focus on the fullness. The things that really matter will bring you more than the things that don't. I slept like a baby with a lighter tummy. I love being gluten free with a lighter tummy and weighing less! I have less joint pain and my back doesn't hurt as much. I am a lot more energized. I never expected this. Joy oh bliss!

I head back home for a New Year's Business Meeting with a potluck extravaganza. Well you had better just forget it if you think out of luck you will find something at the potluck gluten free. Potlucks by nature are fried chicken, macaroni and cheese and casserole city. Everybody is thinking of creamy and cheesy and hot. I guarantee you if it is creamy and dreamy that there is flour in it. I don't have time to ask everyone is there flour in your dish? The world is not adapting to you. You are adapting to it. Tip number one. Do not arrive hungry to a potluck.

This was a business meeting and we had work to do. So I played it smart. Rule number one of deprivation station is to eat your most favorite healthy filling meal before you get there. I had an avocado, walnut, chicken, red pepper salad with lime dressing. Oh so good! The content of my entrepreneurs group was fabulous. So I feasted on that instead of the dishes before me. I have come a long way from cheating on myself with bad boyfriend foods. I got over it! Got out of my own way! I feel better, calmer, more adjusted. I am more present to the possibility of wellness and wholeness with connection to my mind, body, soul and dreams!

Gluten Free Friends

"Friendship is born at that moment when one person says to another, "What! You too? I thought I was the only one."

C.S. Lewis

The whole world is full of gluten free freaks like me. They are everywhere. The grocery store... even Instagram. That is my favorite place to see recipes in an Insta second with pics, videos and solutions from non-gluten lovers like myself. Just good to know we are not alone in a world full of bread lovers. We had a snowstorm last week. What does a gal do who is gluten and dairy free when everyone is stocking up on bread and milk? Yes I discovered I am dairy intolerant. What is happening here? Well thank God for Forager Cashew Yogurt. Amazing. My next favorite is Cocovi Yogurt with 20 billion probiotics. This stuff is living young coconut. I never even heard of it but my favorite store Fresh Thyme has it all. Thank God for chocolate, no they can't take that away from me. Lots of gluten free chocolate brownie mixes out there.

A lady made my day when I was at the Italian deli where they served gluten free pasta. I was chatting with a gal who worked there. She shared with me that she became gluten free because of inflammation. We talked about how hard it was as we longingly stared over the pastries from the best place in the county. Chocolate Bavarian Cream looking at me right between the eyes making my lips smack and eyes water. You're killing me right? She told me about cassava flour and how it matched with chocolate so well. Mmmm.

I never knew I was craving this so much a gluten free friend to embark on my journey. It is just nice to know I am not alone in my gluten free world here. For us gluten free freaks it can be a lonely battle. There are others out there in the world just like me. I told her I started a book about this and she cheered me on. That is just what I needed today. We all need cheerleaders. You got this. You can do this. It is not the end of the world as you know it. It is just the beginning. Change embarks upon other change. Out of pain emerges glory I believe. Better health awaits you and new friends who share your journey who get it.

The Lifestyle That NO Longer Serves Me

"Sometimes the very thing you are afraid of doing, is the very thing that will set you free."

Robert Tew

This is it... the mindset hack that will change your life. Something about your lifestyle, your health, your habits have led you here and they no longer serve you. Something is not working right? I venture to bet it is more than just the digestion and the flour right? It could be high levels of stress, career imbalance, family disconnects and even pressure etc. It all piles on and I am sure our tummies can't take it. Even putting ourselves profoundly last can do a number on you!

I can tell you that gluten free is a huge revolutionary mindset adjustment! But if you wrap your head around it first then you have got this. The battle begins in the mind. As you can tell by my freaky behavior at the beginning of the book when I DIDN'T HAVE IT. I realize as I am surfing the aisles for gluten free flours that so many areas of my life need a makeover. Not just my eating habits, but my cooking skills, meal prep and time management to name a few. I need choices that serve the big life I want to live. A life where my passions and dreams come true and I break free of all constraints and limitations imposed only in my mind.

You know why they call it a mindset? That is because our minds are so powerful and they get fixed upon something and it forms almost like a fortress or impenetrable force. But imagine if you will crossing the mind over the sea of doubt, self-pity or fear to the powerful place of acceptance and embracing your life full on. You have an amazing life. Gluten can't rob you of that. Your life is created by you. Everything in it.

Once you set your mind on health, well-being, connection, fun, purpose and balance you are truly free. You embrace what is powerful about your life and run from what is not.

Gluten Free is Not a Dirty Word

"I am not telling you it's going to be easy- I am telling you it's going to be worth it."

Art Williams

Ever feel like you have to announce yourself to the world and you sound sterile when you say I have gone gluten free. People look at you sad like the baby was born dead, you are reproductively barren or something. It is because they have no connection to it. No point of reference. It just sounds miserable to them. It sounds like a burden, a cross to be born, and a challenge. I will tell you a secret. It is a bridge to a better life. A life where you get to run the show, pain free, energy filled and more. Rich with possibility and promise while you live full out and own all your power. The secret in life is ultimately that anyway. You don't give your power away ever to a food, an opinion of others, nothing. Today I walked around a gym four or five times and three months ago I could barely walk around it once because I had so much inflammation and joint pain.

For me to walk around the gym with a spring in my step is worth all the trips to the store to buy gluten-free flours and all the things I couldn't ever put on my plate again. This was off my plate. The joint pain was bad. So I traded one thing for another. Not a bad switch. Give up a little flour, some leaven, something called yeast and I get my life step back. Fast forward 3 months and I am going out dancing again, something that was not even a desire due to joint pain and just feeling crappy.

The life I had chosen no longer served me, so I created a whole new life for myself; Gluten free, pain free, inflammation free, drama free and disease free. Freedom is worth the sacrifice it takes to get there and the uphill battle to climb. One change is worth a mountain of regrets over what you never tried. Freedom for me means more mobility in my joints, more possibility, and more ability to access whatever I want in this life.

When I want I get to rise, to climb, to soar, to travel, to dance, to jump to salsa and to tango. I have CREATED FOR MYSELF A NEW CAPACITY. I HAVE STRETCHED MY CAPACITY. I can do what I want when I want. Nothing is hindering me or restricting me. That my friend is worth giving up anything for. See it is a mindset shift for sure. Letting go of the flour, the gluten, the sad story about what I can't have has given me a new story in life. If you're struggling to adjust to gluten free, do some soul searching for your why. Hang your Why up on the wall. Seriously, do you want to dance again, travel more, or lose 50 lbs.?   Connect to your why with a vision board. Put it somewhere you will see it daily. The closet, the mirror, or the frig!

What are You Hiding? What are You Pretending?

"When I am hungry I eat what I love, When I am bored, I do something I love, When I am lonely, I connect with someone I love, When I am sad, I remember that I am loved."

Michelle May

Will the real you step forward please? Yes, I am talking to you. Halfway into my gluten challenge I realize there is a different me underneath all the layers of lies and bad choices that I have hidden from even myself. I lost about 15 lbs. and have more clarity. But what I mean is even deeper than that. I have been hiding out in life covering up the real person beneath carbs, excess body fat, depleted energy levels and more lies about myself.

The carbs, the sugar, just kept me safe under it all. It allowed me to play small and keep up the false pretense that I was unworthy and not enough. A new and different person is emerging. A freer soul. A truer version of me. A lot of my old clothes fit now. I have some pretty amazing clothes too. That feels so tremendous. I want to leave my mark on the world and I almost gave it up for the love of a carb, a mere potato of my soul, a dry crumbly piece of bread. We all have incredible dreams inside each one of us that we cover up in lies. The lie we tell ourselves about who we really are. Have you accepted the lie? Lived with it so long you don't know any better? Giving up gluten has revealed to my soul the unbelief about my true soul's worth that I let stick to my soul for 56 years like a thick glutinous mass of paste, suffocating my dreams and potential. Smothering my offering to life of all my zest, beauty and passion. It is time to surrender the lie finally.

I step into a new space. I claim my space with all the champions I never felt good enough to be in the room with before. Now the room belongs to me. I am a champion and I rise to claim my birthright; what I was put here on this Earth to do from the beginning of time. There is no fear that will keep me from succeeding. No loss that can separate me from rising now. I step into my destiny. She is mine. She is come. She was waiting for me to make this decision so patiently in order for me to become all I was created for.

What are You Addicted To?

"The three most harmful addictions are heroin, carbohydrates, and a monthly salary."

Nassim Nicholas Taleb

Food is kind of like an addiction. Our habits over years and years have created our cravings, what we love and think we can't live without. Sometimes when we fill our mouths and stuff our bellies we are filling them with untruth. Addiction to the lesser more comfortable version of ourselves. The easy way out. Addiction to comforting our losses and not truly healing them.

What if we were addicted to our success? I might have to face what lies underneath all the masks and cover up. Some hurt, some buried pain, and some stuffed unresolved grief over a lifetime of losses. I think it would be worth it all for the real version of me to arise from underneath the ruin and rubble. I have always been a carbaholic, kind of an emotional eater. But when we confront what we are most afraid of it no longer has any power over us. We don't need to hide or pretend anymore.

Let the lie out. The untruth about your soul. In order to end the addiction it has to come out. I lost 20 lbs. now. I have been trying to lose that for years always telling myself I can't do it. Well when gluten hits my belly I can't do that. So giving it up has been easy. Finally, the truth emerges. I am not my losses. I am not my fears. I am not less than. I am not my performance in life. I am not my job resume. I am not what those closest to me think of me. I am not left behind in life, alone because of those who went ahead.

The truth is I am an amazing, connected, loveable, worthy, transparent, soul; in process, never perfect, on her way to glory, getting better, emerging, developing, becoming, learning and transforming. The truth is I have so much to offer, so much to give to the world and so do you. I have limited myself with the tiny little lies about what I couldn't do. I have acted helpless in areas of my life like weight loss, life balance, and business. I have settled for a lesser version of all my capabilities.

But now this caterpillar emerges from her cocoon, the one she spun of self-protection. Alas, she is a glorious butterfly. That is the beauty of life; we are always becoming, developing, ever arriving if we allow ourselves to open our wings and expand. Once you become the butterfly there is no going back to being a caterpillar. You just can't. The butterfly has the freedom to take flight and that you must. In every area of your life it is time to be addicted to your success. Success meaning health, well-being, connected relationships, living your passions and dreams, acknowledging you're a spiritual being with a need to connect to God and not going this life alone. You have arrived my friend on the other side when you just begin to let go.

I find it interesting that gluten is a binding agent. What is it that holds us together when we are faced with having to surrender something we don't want to? I find my faith every releasing the things I buried for years deep inside: Unable to release on my own. My undeniably loveable creator has allowed me to face when I was ready. So when I have had fear on my life's journey I have a little exercise I like to do. It is opening up my hands to release what is in them and asking God to place in them what is in His hands instead.

I thought becoming gluten free would be the death of me. Instead it has been the burst of new life, kind of like being born again if you'll excuse the cliché. When your born again your old man is made new in Christ. You become a new creature. The old has passed away. So the girl who loved bread, pasta, raw cookie dough has passed away and a gal who loves more in life has sprung forth. The girl who loves and embraces all life has to offer. If I can beat this gluten thing, I know you can too!

This journey has been more about taking back every dream. You know if I don't take them back they will just die inside me. Imagine that for yourself. I don't want my dreams lying dead on the doorway of my tombstone, do you? We all have it inside ourselves: the best version of ourselves. Fully unrestricted, unbounded, unhindered, and relentless. Unstoppable you. That's right you have just entered a new season of your life that connects you to more possibilities than ever before.

Heal the body and you set free the soul. Be a dream catcher if you will. One who attracts great abundance in their life. Where do you begin? Don't just make your gluten free grocery list. There is more soul food that you need. Make the dream catcher list. The dreams you want to produce in your life and draw in both big and small.

I have a gorgeous dress in my closet that didn't fit before I became gluten free and now it does. I forgot what it felt like to be pretty, sexy, joint pain and brain fog left me feeling dull and lifeless. I was exhausted most of the time due to not sleeping. My mojo, my get up and go was gone, all spent on chronic inflammation in my body. Here is my list of what this gluten free freak is attracting into her life.

1. Unlimited energy
2. Ability to travel and see those I love
3. More heads turning in my elegant dress
4. A series of successes that beat out the series of failures that crushed my soul
5. The love of my life
6. A large biz platform
7. Extra cash to give away
8. Dancing the tango again
9. Climbing stairs without the freaky, creaky drama in my joints
10. Inspiring the world
11. Imparting faith to those who lost theirs

Kind of a tall list I know, but remember I am a freak. I am a stand out of the range of normalcy. The unreachable reach, the ungettable get that is my stand. The love, success that is beyond your reach is just right there; it comes after you are free from whatever has weighed you down for so many years. Somebody has got to stand for it in this crazy game of life. What would you let go of on your plate right now to free up some space to create something new and completely different? Something that may never have been possible before.

I visualize in my imagination life being like two circles. To me they symbolize plates. One plate is what I want to let go of: fear, excuses, lies, limiting beliefs, bad choices, sabotage, and resistance to change, restrictions, and sad stories. The other plate is what I want to create more of: energy, balance, freedom, joy sexiness, intimacy, vulnerability and relationships.

Let's celebrate you! Celebrating because I have always loved a party as it involves my two favorite things: food and people. You know the more you celebrate your successes the more successes you have. Beating yourself up never creates anything. Acknowledging yourself creates more success. Have you tried some new recipes yet? That is great. Have you added avocados, coconut oil or healthy gut foods? Have you feasted on dark green leafy bitter foods like Brussel sprouts, kale, arugula, collard greens or Bok choy, mustard greens or turnips? Your body loves you for it.

I think we have lost the connection between our habits, what we put in our mouths, grab and go and the fruit it produces in our bodies and all of our lives. If you ask anyone, do you love yourself? Of course the answer is yes I do. But if you observe what we shove in our mouths or how we say we are too busy to cook or prepare meals it reveals a huge disconnect between our intentions and our reality. Our brains are on autopilot. Have you ever grabbed lunch at the gas station? Nothing wrong here but we are not cars to be refueled by a pump on the run. Our refueling takes some time, thought and definite care or our vehicles, our only sole irreplaceable vehicle will run down and we can't replace most parts.

Breakdowns and Breakthroughs

"Everybody is breaking grounds, but you must breakthrough."

Israelmore Ayiyor

My heart breaks for you if you like me are missing out on some of life's best and most beautiful moments because of your gluten allergy. I have too. I am a survivor. A pusher if you will. I can't stop here to dwell on it. I must press forward. We were all born to overcome. Today I wanted to go blackberry picking with my niece and I had gotten cross contaminated and my joints swelled up so I couldn't even walk around the house. Someone gave me some sausage at a vineyard. Really? Taken out by a tiny piece of meat. This is depressing.

The night before I was at a vineyard enjoying some of the most amazing guitar music on the planet and my sacroiliac joint flared up. This happens to me when I eat something with gluten. It is my worst reaction to my food sensitivity. I went from loving the moment, the sheer joy, bliss, of the night to such discomfort I wanted to leave.

Life happens and freaking things happen, but no we are not freaks. We are still loveable in our most painful moments. Yes we are. You may feel like you inconvenience others but you are not an inconvenience. Perhaps some areas of my life still need a makeover. More stretching, more rest, more water, the list is endless. The one thing I got really present to is the social aspect of eating for a gathering. These are new friends and they want to share what is on their plate or in their picnic with me. The most scrumptious hearth baked pizzas being served there. People bringing sausage and cheese trays and sharing wine. Snacks so delicious that I have to refuse. The best thing to do is come prepared with what everyone else is feasting on. But I forgot. I forgot to think of me. I forgot to think of what I need right now in this moment. Time to change my story.

The world is full of gluten free crackers and cheeses, sausages and dairy free cheese dips. Even nonalcoholic sangria. I would have been happier if I could participate in the party at my own level instead of staring at the devil of denial because I couldn't have any. It is not fun to not have what everyone else is having at the party. But life is too short to miss out on people and parties just because we are crying over the food.

I truly was present to it all. The music was sensational, Jupiter rising in the night sky, The Big Dipper, a crowd on a hill, air so fresh, music so mellow for the soul. The moments were rich. The experience of being with everyone on a long blazing summer night, crickets chirping, charcoal smells rising from the hearth oven behind me.
If I could relive this day over- should I have stayed home to avoid the embarrassment of my flare up, my joint going out? I am entitled to experience all of life and everything she throws my way... The good, the bad and the ugly.

If I can take a moment and hit the pause button on my remote perhaps I need more of this. More relaxation, more connection and excitement. My day could use more rest. When our bodies have inflammation and flare ups the healing occurs in the let go. In the be still moments. In the down time. We need good old rest and relaxation, to chill, take a time out from the madness. I was engaged

31

in great conversation before my flare up. I enjoy other people with no agenda, just tuning in to their frequency.

The performer changed hand selected guitars over ten times in his performance. I never saw anything like it. He knew just one tweak, one octave or different pitch can reach out and grab another's soul. One chord could make a difference in the masterful performance of a lifetime. The masters know it who are the well-seasoned performers that they have made not just a living but a life off this divine knowledge. That's it, my life, my relationships, food planning, rest just need some more tweaking. Just a touch here and a little adjustment there. A little chord change here can lead to glory.

It is up to me to master my life and what is missing to make the whole melody and the entire ballad come out oh so sweet. We need to figure out how to produce the masterful moments in life that indulge us in the very full breath of life with all our senses. Life still has everything to offer you. Don't dwell on the pain, the inconvenience, the sacrifice you have to make. Resist fighting what has been sent your way. We all flow better when we work with ourselves and not against ourselves.

You can create life in the ebb and flow of the pain, the injury, the loss by flowing with it and not against it. Those people, that music they would be missing your presence if you don't show up. Participate when you can and when you are required to pull away just let it be. You can come back stronger and more whole. Your hour is coming when you're free in all the moments of life. It is always a choice how we get to be in every moment. I am still grateful I stood under the stars in pain on an endlessly heat blazing summer night and heard the most amazing music. Life reveals its glory when we simply show up.

Mindfulness and Eating

"Every moment nature is serving fresh dishes with the items of happiness. It is our choice to recognize and taste it."

Amit Ray

I think we suffer from mindless eating. A lack of mindful eating. I know I sure did. We just keep doing the same old, same old and don't get the impact on our health. We are creatures of habit. Mindful eating would really empower all of us. Get present to what did I eat today and how did my body feel as a result. Why did I eat what I did? Am I deficient in planning, my own value or life balance etc.? What did I eat in the last 24 hours and how did it affect my sleep, self-talk, energy level, digestion and productivity even?

As I become more mindful I can be aware of what to fix and change. Have a bad day? Feel like you have been hit by a bus? What did you eat most recently? How has the week overall looked? Now shift it. Didn't sleep in the last 24 hours? What have you eaten? Eat something lighter, healthier for dinner and see if you sleep better. In my gluten drama I have had to incorporate gut healing foods. Ginger for digestion, Aloe Vera juice, probiotics, apple cider vinegar etc. Mindful eating can produce more results in every area of our lives.

I couldn't sleep two nights in a row. I changed what I was eating for dinner and slept like a baby. Our digestion is a sensitive animal that unlocks the mysterious control over lots of areas of our lives. Digestion and sleep impacted by food sensitivities. Yes. I googled it.

Someone else besides me found it to be true if google took note of it. So let's play food detective here and see if you have other food allergies or flare ups.

My Sacroiliac joint had pain and was going out on me regularly. A wise soul asked me what I was eating before each flare up. I changed what I was eating and stopped getting the flare ups. The mindful eating has been a revolutionary breakthrough for me. Our mind is a powerful force. What do you want to create more of in life? The "ness" implies full of. What do you want your life full of: playfulness, sexiness, completeness, greatness, happiness or gratefulness etc.?

Find what is missing in an area of your life and create more of it. You might need more fun in your life, too much stress, too much energy around chronic problems with money, marriage or kids etc. Adding balance brings breakthroughs. I guarantee you when you are out of balance in one area everything backs up or clogs up. Fun reduces stress, playfulness can create sexiness which could improve your marriage. A friend and I weekly ask each other what we are looking forward to. It is a great possibility to create with someone to remind ourselves we can have good, pleasure, fun, escape, play and bust the stress, anxiety and grip of all the negative over our soul. I challenge you to make a list of what you are looking forward to. If you don't have anything on the list, try getting with a friend and being held accountable to come up with small things every week you look forward to.

Healing the Core

"Broken people are beautiful. They have to put themselves back together every day."

Robert Tew

I was told that the guts layers run deep, so inflammation in the gut can take more time to heal the stomach lining if it is damaged. It is an elimination diet that I need to clean out my gut for a deep healing and cleansing. I have been practicing intermittent fasting where you eat only through a certain window of a few hours like a 10 hour window. It sounds confusing but it actually is simple. You just don't eat or fast breakfast and begin your eating window later like 1:00 in the afternoon. This allows your gut the opportunity to rest from digesting food. I experienced some tremendous results when practicing this for 30 days.

When the gut is backed up than the brain is also backed up. I experienced a clearing of what I like to call brain fog. I no longer felt fuzzy but sharp and clear in the mornings and more productive. You ever see your kitchen drain when it has a deep clog, nothing is getting through that sucker! You have to go get that special wrench get under the sink and torque and twist that special place to release all that stuff backed up in the sink. Same is true of our colons.

What runs deep in our cores may also need a healing such as our false or limiting beliefs about ourselves, our anxieties, our fears and sensitivities to stress. The breakdown in our lives need addressing. Wherever there has been a breakdown we need a breakthrough. Has there been a breakdown in an area of life for you? For me it has been many areas. I found the Holy Spirit helping me breakthrough when I couldn't break through on my own power.

God the ultimate healer doing what only He can do in my body, mind and spirit tearing down my own walls of resistance to every fear and failure. I found prayer to be a place of healing for me, sweet release and freedom to express all the cries of my heart to the one who made it and knows it so well. Prayer is not a religious act, it is just a conversation, a communication spoken to a person. The person of The Father, The Son and the Holy Spirit.

It is in my inner chamber, like the walls of my gut, communicating my innermost needs and desires and deepest felt feelings to the one who made me. You can hide them, but they are there longing to be expressed and received by your creator. He made us surely He can heal us. I believe He communicates with us in a still small voice like a whisper even. He talks to our gut, a place we know, we just know we have heard him accept us, love us, free us and restore us and ultimately our lives. He is my answer to every breakdown.

Spirituality: The Deepest Core

In John 6:35 Jesus said, "I am the bread of life, He who comes to me will not hunger anymore. Neither will He thirst anymore." In a day and age where self-sufficiency is praised it is hard to be spiritual. Spirituality implies a need for someone greater outside of ourselves. What is spirituality I ask myself? What is missing in my spiritual life if I added it the presence thereof would make my life richer, fuller and more complete?

I think spirituality is connecting to a higher purpose than just ourselves. It is connecting to faith in the unseen. It is connecting heart to heart, soul to soul, and pain to pain. If my fellow man suffers than I suffer too because we are ultimately all connected. I am not just here all alone on this planet to strive and struggle. There is a greater purpose. Spirituality is being in connection with my fellow man, suffering alongside with him or her to feel their pain as well as my own. It is serving in a larger community for the greater good. It is sacrifice like Jesus portrayed it on the cross. Spirituality is a sense of being open, connected of service and available. Selflessness.

Spirituality is my adding value to the lives of others without getting anything in return. Realizing I am not just a physical body. I have a spirit inside of me. Am I growing to become more of this selfless creature or am I becoming more self-absorbed? When I seek to encourage others I feel the life coming back to me. Spirituality is sharing my gifts with the world, what resonates with me, my powerful truths, lessons learned from failure make me stronger when I let them out.

How can I create more connection to God if I have been cut off? It all begins with a conversation. A rant if you will. Let's try an opener. Any opening line will do. Whose line is it anyway? God already knows. He is just waiting to hear from you.

Stress Buster Wheel

Sensitivity to Stress

"Some of the most beautiful things worth having in your life come wrapped in a crown of thorns."

Shannon Adler

I think some of us are more sensitive to stress than others. It can be our personality. We are just not wired for drama. We need a certain amount of stability and serenity to maintain our sanity. I am like that. You know some flowers wither in the heat earlier. That is ok, it doesn't mean you are weaker. You just were created for something other than what you might be currently manifesting in your life. You have the power to fix it, to change it, to make your life reborn if you will in areas of breakdown.

How's your coping mechanisms? How's your support level from those around you? How's your vulnerability factor to let others know your needs at your most stressful times? We need to focus on an anchor of change, hope, resiliency, meditation, quietness, and breakthrough. Sometimes we can just add something to our lives and that will help. You can add fun, vacation, support, passions, hobbies, and relaxation, rituals that let you release and calm down.

Which one of these can you create for yourself? Our brain exists in a loop of thoughts and patterns, that's how anxiety gets you. You wake up feeling the resistance to the same stress from yesterday. A small ritual can change that. I got up early one a.m. and completely altered my routine. It felt like my world opened up to everything else that might be possible. I discovered a new park with a lake in my town where I could go just be quiet and wake up slowly sitting in the sun. Then I felt exhilarated completely different, energized for the day and not anticipating the cares I went to bed with the night before. Take a look at what is missing in your life and create something new from the Stress Wheel that helps you take on your life in a more powerful way. Listen to your gut. You were made for more. More than just work, work, work.

If you want more time or travel freedom in your life it is a good idea to examine what is working and what is not working. Purge the latter and embrace the former. Freedom allows expansion in an area of our lives. The multiplication of what you dream of. The abundance of good generated by your own carefully laid out plans and intentions. This is your turning point. The point in which you will deem that the miraculous is even possible. We create our lives by our mindset, our choices, and our decisions.

This is a choice on your wheel, like when you were a kid and you spin the spinner to see what you win. As an adult you get to choose the winning spin every time. Why don't we? Sometimes we just think we can't get there. Don't like where you landed in the game of life? Spin again! Lack energy, zest, get up and go you once had? I did too baby! It is so much harder at the age of 56. We can all steal another hour here or there to create what we want on our journey. You can have whatever you want in life. What do you need? More time, rest, money, energy? You can create it for yourself.

What is a shift you can manifest this week to create more money, more energy, more fun, free time or family time? You may need to start a side business, go back to school, and get an accountability partner to get your but to the gym or spend a day planning your meals. In the end it is well worth it. Don't believe the lie that you are stuck in your current situation and nothing will change. Own your power.

You can create money freedom, time freedom, and energy freedom. You have to map it out and make a plan of how to get there. Write it down, in bite size manageable chunks and commit to your plan. If you write it down you are more likely to accomplish it. Set an end date. Carve out time in your routine. If you are going to start a side hustle to make more money and you can devote ten hours a week to it that is a beginning. If you can do it from 6 to 7pm that makes it even more likely to happen. Make a ritual around when you will take on this new habit. First thing in the morning or late at night?

I wrote my first book only on the weekends because I was so sleep deprived. Whatever you got baby will get you there. It all begins with the first step. I could only write on the weekends due to my job challenges and tired brain. I eventually got my book finished in over a year. You can do this! You can take your life to the next level. Life will get in the way if you don't make a concrete plan and write it on the wall. Lewis Howes wrote himself a certificate of achievement in regards to his first high paid speech for thousands of dollars before it ever happened. Our minds tend to gravitate toward whatever is on the wall in front of us. We get inspired and decide to create a way to make it happen.

The Possibility of Connection

"The need for connection and community is primal as fundamental as the need for air, water and food."

Dean Omish

Are you connected in life? Do you have people you count on? Are you as connected as you possibly can be? Do you crave more connection in your concoction of life? The crazy, the sane and the mundane. When we spend time with others we become a stronger version of ourselves. We flourish. We thrive.

Connection is a possibility we create in life. We reach for it. You can find it anywhere. A meet up. A book club. A coffee house. A Facebook group for those fellows likeminded as you. People are connecting on Facebook sharing their deepest struggles with others because they are looking for answers to all of life's proverbial questions; dating, writing a book, hungry gals dieting etc. The list goes on and on. I love to see people rally around others when they express a struggle. Let others rally around you.

Find your tribe as they say. I remember being invited to a wedding in Africa and over 1000 people were invited. The whole village. Why? Because they were all connected to the one soul. They belong together at the wedding of one of their fellow tribe members. So do we. We belong to each other. I think we have lost our sense of connection in the hustle and bustle and the rat race of life. It used to be your community that came to save you in a crisis.

Do you have a community you dance with and cry with? If you have a problem, share it. If you have a solution, offer it. Gluten free even has a society. Why not get all the support you need in life? Harvard Medical School did a study that showed women with breast cancer who were connected were more likely to recover quicker.

Relationships Define Your Inner Circle

"Celebrate the people in your life who are there because they love you for no other reason than because you are YOU."

Mandy Hale

Research studies conducted on people who lived long lives reveal a common factor is their quality of relationships they possess over time. Life can turn on a dime but the people who stick with you through thick and thin are the ones who enrich your lives. It is better shared together. All of it, the good, the bad and the ugly.

I have a coaching exercise for you. Try it with me. Close your eyes and visualize those closest to you in your life. This is called your inner circle. Who is in your inner circle? Are they cheering you on? Do they stand for you in crisis? Have you let the right people in? I am not talking about those in physical proximity to you, more so the emotional proximity created by sharing intimate desires, goals and demises.

Now visualize who is in the outer circle? Who do you want to bring from the outer circle to the inner circle? Is someone misplaced in your life? A family member you need to forgive or you keep at a distance out of fear of being hurt or misunderstood. This is a powerful exercise if you ask yourself the right questions. A key question is have I blocked out some people in my inner circle? Is it time to let them in closer? What would the rest of my life be like if I were more vulnerable and transparent? Maybe there are business partners or acquaintances out there you can bring in. Maybe even people you haven't met yet. Who stands for us in our inner circle of life is ultimately up to us. We choose, we create. Choose love over fear. Intimacy over being safe. Freedom over being alone.

Some questions to ask yourself?

1. Who is in your inner circle?
2. Do they challenge you?
3. Do they love you?
4. How well do they help you through thick and thin?
5. Are the relationships reciprocal? Both sides benefiting from being in relationship together?
6. Who is in your outer circle?
7. Anyone in the outer circle you think ultimately might need to be in the inner circle? Can you bring them in? If not what is holding you back from having the best of the best stand by your side in life?
8. Do you cling to false beliefs about what you deserve to have in life?
9. Are there any limiting beliefs holding you back from experiencing a truly empowering inner circle of friends?
10. What shifts in your thinking need to occur to experience all you deserve at the highest level?
11. Are there any toxic people in your inner circle that you need to have boundaries with? Can you place them in the outer circle?

Outer Circle Questions

1. Who is in your outer circle?
2. How often do you communicate with all the people in your

life in a reciprocal way expressing what you truly desire and how you can help each other along the journey?

3. How can you more effectively communicate with those in your life? Put it on the calendar.
4. What is one thing you would like everyone in your life to know, but maybe are afraid to tell or procrastinate telling them? Do you express your heartfelt needs that you have?
5. Do you have a weak outer circle?
6. Do you need to expand your social circles?
7. Do you need a larger circle of connection to accomplish goals and business and dreams you have? What is stopping you from realizing these goals?
8. Are you naturally drawn towards the people who bring out the best in your life?
9. Do you need any different kind of people in your circle? People who are more successful, more driven, or more balanced?
10. What do you bring to the table of relationships for others to feast from? Are you sharing and contributing to the highest capacity you can, feasting on the richness of all your relationships?

They say in life that we are the sum total of the five people closest to us. So if you look at those in your inner circle what does that say about you and where you are headed? Can you let someone in who stretches your capacity? Who you are becoming just by the proximity of who they already are. You attract people into your life. Is there a way you can be resisting attracting greatness? As we evolve on our journeys in life our relationships change over time. I give you permission to adjust the circles in your life to reflect the quality of life you want as a desired outcome.

Geography and proximity do not determine your inner circle. You can have the most powerful person in your inner circle who lives far away and you create the ways you connect to stay connected. FaceTime, phone calls, texting and just being present and connected to even those at a distance who bring us joy can bring you deep satisfaction. Those who nurture the very bone marrow of our existence are worth the fight of overcoming distance, stress in life to keep them close throughout a lifetime.

They will always be the champion in your corner fighting for you every time life throws you a curve ball. Those closest to us make up our identity. Our DNA if you will of purpose, passion, clarity, stability, and resiliency. Our inner core is a permeable force in our lives that allows us to become as we absorb and soak up another's life energy. We co-create life with them, they become the source of our powerhouse. Like the superheroes in Avengers Endgame when you are up against the wall and facing the strongest weapons formed against you, remember you are as powerful as the sum of the five people closest to you.

Reciprocity

"Abundance is a dance with reciprocity – what we can give, what we can share, and what we can receive in the process."

Terry Tempest Williams

What kind of relationships do you have? Are they mutually beneficial? My favorite movie is called Les Intouchables, with French subtitles. It is about a very wealthy man who becomes a paraplegic. He can't keep a caregiver because he is so difficult to deal with. He keeps firing them or they quit. One fine day in walks a strong street smart man who can't find a job. He has experienced a tough go of it living in the hard school of knocks. What ensues as the story unfolds in a most unlikely friendship between two men very different who come from completely opposite walks of life.

The friendship evolves over what they have to learn from each other; mutually exclusive life lessons only they can bring to the table. I loved this story because it was a delightful surprise and not predictable. It taught me what true reciprocity was. The rich man needs someone who will stand up to him and call him out on his crap. Everyone in his life has been too afraid to tell him the truth. The street smart dude needs someone to teach him a few hard lessons where he has let the chip on his shoulder interfere with his outlook on life.

Our relationships don't need to include people who have grown up where we did or who are just like us. The dynamic just needs to be reciprocal. A relationship like that will bond you together with someone over the course of a lifetime and bring you both the healthiest outcomes. If you find yourself always a giver or always a taker than focus on shifting your energy to be something different.

Don't resist letting very different people in your life. You can learn the most from people least like you. It is out of our comfort zone to let people in who make more money or talk to us straight up no holds barred, but it is the only way we can grow. Perhaps we can confront our own limitations as we let others get close and stop hiding or pretending to ourselves but fully uncover truth about who we can ultimately become.

Intimate Conversations in Your Inner Circle

"I wonder if this is how people always get close. They heal each other's wounds; they repair the broken skin."

Lauren Oliver

Whoever is in your inner circle closest to you gives you your power. How vulnerable are you to these people? I confess I have a fear of going to the doctor and I am highly resistant and stubborn about it. I had to tell someone this to process it and walk through it. I was hiding behind my fear and unwillingness to confront my problem. I just wanted the pain to go away.

Saying it out loud to someone I trusted showed up powerfully for me. She told me I need to go to the doctor. I went back and forth telling her I don't want to go. I am afraid to go. She told me about a cousin who refused to go and came down with colon cancer and died in a few months' time. So in facing our worst fear sometimes we need a push, to see our most probable certain future if we don't do something about it.

All I could see was my fear, I never thought about the rest of it. I couldn't see the forest for the trees so to speak. The end of the road. Anxiety put blinders on my vision so it wasn't 20/20. I broke out in a rash the other day which looks like it fits the description of celiac disease. Celiac is a more serious form of GF and has severe consequences like malnutrition that can lead to rotten teeth and bones and falls even. Some people may not even know they have it.

My conversation with my good friend helped me process my fear of the doctor and put it in a larger perspective.

I began to think of all the good things doctors have done for me. When I was 40 a doctor caught a growth called a Schwanoma on an X-ray that saved my life. Another doctor sat me down and gave me a vast education about lowering my blood pressure naturally by weight loss, diet and cardiovascular exercise. They gave me another chance when I thought I couldn't do it. Shortly after that I joined a boxing gym and my high blood pressure began to go down. Nine Rounds Boxing Gym kicked my excuses and high blood pressure to the curb.

I realized that my anxiety about not going to the doctor was keeping me in a holding pattern of not moving forward fully with my life. I don't have all the information here about Celiac disease. Anxiety is a wicked thing. It wants to grip us like a heavy blanket over our will. We can't let it. It has lies for us about our future and who we will be.

But we are stronger than the anxiety. So this precious conversation got me unstuck. I tell myself I can go see the doctor and talk to someone who is an expert and more experienced than me. The anxiety is not going to win this game. I am and so can you in any area you need. Have conversations with those in your inner circle who can help you.

Anxiety: Fear is a Liar

Bound up tight and locked up, still small like our bellies full of gluten. Anxiety is a glass cage we live inside; a prison where we are locked behind the walls of our minds. Our minds holding us down that we can only go so far in life. We feel like we are stuck and can't make it all the way down the road.

The gluten drama creates anxiety because it gets in our nervous system. We need a detox to get it out completely. A deep cleanse if you will. But what about a mind cleanse. A purging of our old way of thinking about who we are and where we can go in life. Don't listen to the anxiety coming from your gut. It is your bodies way of telling you to eat differently and there is some inflammation.

The opposite of anxiety is being completely present and free in the moment. The best way to create this is through an exercise of gratitude and creation of who we are going to be in the moment.

Be present and be Grateful

We have a lot to be thankful for every day. Life is a precious gift. Never take it for granted. Don't let there be a disconnect because of the added pain. Try this exercise with me. Today I am most grateful for these three things. I am staying present to those around me by_____. I am reaching out to friends and loved ones today by_____. I chose to create myself as _____. (Unstoppable, love, power, passion, etc.)

Life's Pleasures and Passions

"Drink without getting drunk. Love without suffering jealousy, Eat without overindulging. Never argue and once in a while with great discretion, misbehave."

Dan Buettner

Food has always been one of my greatest, most delightful and richest indulgences and pleasures in life. Chocolate, dark with sea salt and creamy caramel, you know... The explosion of senses in the taste buds. The creamy, the sweet, the delectable, the desirable making the brain eclipse with an explosion of ultimate satisfaction all coming from food, glorious food. Our brains are wired like a circuit and it's incredibly difficult to unwire. That is why changing a diet of a lifetime is so challenging. We feel helpless to overcome cravings, peer pressure, social pressure, emotional needs etc. Habits that are engrained in the very fiber of our soul. How can we win the fight?

What we fight the will with is our purpose. Replace you will with your why. Why can't I eat all of this scrumptious stuff? Not just gluten and dairy but sugar and spice and everything- oh so nice. It is because you have a greater purpose in life, a reason to be healthier for. A destiny to obtain. A driven passionate powerful purpose. When we are connected to our purpose we can conquer the demons of our diet by discovering and diving into the delight of our destiny.

Why were you put here on Earth? What is the one thing you would regret not doing leaving planet Earth? What is your mission? Have you ever considered writing your destiny statement? Those who are intentional, purposeful, deliberate ultimately create the best outcomes. How do I write a destiny statement? It begins in your core. Your core values, beliefs, passions and ultimate purpose in life. You can make yourself uncomfortable for a greater purpose.

Perhaps discovering the purpose you were born for would provide the extreme motivation to take back your diet. Clean all that inflammation and junk out of your gut and the correlation it has to the rest of your life. Your destiny should drive you, compel you forward, and inspire your socks off. It should ultimately be the reason you get up every day. I challenge you to write your destiny statement and decorate it and frame it on your wall.

What if you don't know your destiny statement? Start with what you do know. You know your strengths. You can build a lifetime off those. Characteristics such as kindness, (the Kind Bar) humor (Steve Martin) Connection (Oprah Winfrey) Being a mouthpiece (Maria Shriver).

God made you with talents, character traits, drives and desires. You are a deliberate masterpiece. Make a list of your top traits and see if those might become part of your destiny statement.

To get you started reflect on which of these you mostly are:

Funny, Focused, Scientific, Analytical

Humorous, Motivating, Comforting, Compassionate

Overcoming, Creative, Musical, Empathetic,

Silly, Speaker of Truth, Intentional, Deliberate

Creative, Passionate, Connected, Free

Smart, Puzzle solver, Problem solver, Designer

Artistic, Musical, Verbal, Social

Athletic, Articulate, Abundant,

Kind, Compassionate, Leader, Mercy

Rescuer, Truth lover, Bold, Fierce

Loyal, Committed, Energetic, Steady

Calm, Centered, Collected, Decisive

Thoughtful, Willing, Sweet, Sure

Confident, Trailblazer, Way maker, Destiny maker

Let me share with you my destiny statement:

To use my gifts of courage, motivation and words to inspire the masses to transform their lives, take back their worst fears and fail forward.

To use my talents of talk, encouragement and my life story of overcoming fear to empower others to lead the best life they can ever imagine, championing their destiny and overcoming the worst in life to create the best most beautiful outcomes.

To create connections, conversations that release a chain reaction in others, an explosion of growth where they completely fall in love with their lives and are compelled to fulfill their destiny.

I wrote without judgment just letting the words come out in different ways to see what resonates with my soul the most. Keeping my destiny statement in front of me will help me to press forward and stay focused despite the challenges.

The exercise might seem silly at first but trust me it will drive you forward toward attaining more of what you are good at ultimately in life. Our passions are our purpose. It is a win, win.

So again if you are finding it challenging take your strengths and make a statement about how you can use them in the world if you had no limitations or restrictions on you. What do you love in life? What are you most passionate about? What brings you pleasure when you see others get something accomplished?

Take the next step and just begin with your ultimate vision in mind. A destiny will require everything from you. What will it cost you to fulfill your destiny? Our superheroes like Sexy Scarlett Johansen or Iconic Iron man can tell you it will cost them sacrificing everything. But I want you to get present to the ultimate perspective here. What will it cost you if you don't fulfill your destiny?

You will live another version of your life perhaps mediocre. Keep that in mind that the success is worth the struggle. If you have to sacrifice some sleep, some food indulgences, some bad habits, some ego to get out of your own way I guarantee you it is worth it all to fulfill your destiny. Something greater pulls us and compels us to become the best version of ourselves.

What is it going to cost you to become the best version of yourself? The person as you become older you look in the mirror and are most proud to have become. The one staring back at you that you can proudly say you made it! Not someone else's version of success, but yours alone to claim.

Visualize who you are becoming in life and you will become rich even. The hidden gem in life is to focus on the transformational process. Resiliency shines brighter like a diamond to be admired. You know in the mining process of diamonds they all began as a lump of coal. You are becoming beautiful, resilient, strong, formidable, undeniable, unstoppable and mostly a rare thing of beauty.

Circumstances will shift around you but focus on who you are becoming in the process and you will empower yourself to rise from any challenge.

Who AM I Becoming?

These are powerful affirmations I wrote focusing on where I intend to go and grow in my life. Life can be an anxious conundrum trying to figure it all out. Until we arrive, focus on who you are becoming.

I AM BECOMING a person who is highly sought after.

I AM BECOMING a person who has choices at her fingertips.

I AM BECOMING a person who totally trusts her instincts.

I AM BECOMING a person who crushes her fears instead of letting them crush her.

I AM BECOMING a person who laughs in the face of adversity.

I AM BECOMING a person who is powerfully socially connected.

I AM BECOMING a person I won't even recognize a year from now.

I AM BECOMING a stronger more resilient version of myself.

I AM BECOMING a person who loves more generously.

I AM BECOMING a person who learns from the most ridiculous situations.

I AM BECOMING a woman rising to fulfill her destiny.

I AM BECOMING a person you can't say no to.

I AM BECOMING a person with a strong muscular healthy body I worked hard to maintain.

I AM BECOMING a person received and celebrated by the world.

I AM BECOMING a person who closes the gaps on my worst obstacles.

I AM BECOMING a person who contributes with the grandest gestures to those in need.

I AM BECOMING a person highly connected in my community.

I AM BECOMING a person who asks for what she needs until it is manifested.

I AM BECOMING a person who has achieved perfect balance.

I AM BECOMING a person who has time freedom and money freedom.

I AM BECOMING a person who leads and inspires others to do brave acts.

I AM BECOMING a person who manifests possibilities now in this moment.

I AM BECOMING A person who asks better questions from myself others and life.

I AM BECOMING a person who doesn't miss an opportunity, not one.

I AM BECOMING a person who finds a way and makes a way.

I AM BECOMING a person who always has time for people. People are the core of my being.

I AM BECOMING a person who talks to anyone in pursuit of my dreams.

I AM BECOMING a person not afraid of my position in life.

I AM BECOMING A person who asks others to invest in me.

I AM BECOMING a person who gives myself the best of everything in life.

I AM BECOMING a person who gives flight to my dreams.

Vulnerability is the New Strength

To be vulnerable is to be human, real and raw. So raw you may bleed, but in that bleeding of your soul, you become connected to another individual who can make you stronger. We become whole when we reveal the inner part of ourselves, our weaknesses, fears and limitations, our inner core or gut if you will. We tend to see vulnerability as a weakness. It is actually a strength. It makes you known, loved for what you really are. There is no sustainable healing and connection in life when we face difficulties without letting others in to see us and help us. We let others come in and empower us so they can come alongside us to rise up over our adversities.

We are interdependent not codependent. We need each other. How did we become so disconnected, isolated, and separated? Are there areas of our lives where you need to receive help, let others contribute to you, receive advice, receive problem solving or receive strength? Ask yourself to take the risk and open up to those who can contribute to you in a powerful way.

Some of us myself included have very dark moments that others never see, but you quietly triumph over. The news from the doctor, the longstanding bills you can't pay, bankruptcy, divorce, being sued or bullied at work. Shout out to you for enduring, pressing forward and rising up.

In the words of Rocky Balboa… "Let me tell you something you already know. The world isn't all sunshine and rainbows. It's a very mean and nasty place and I don't care how tough you are it will beat you to your knees and keep you there permanently if you let it. You, I, or nobody is going to hit as hard as life. But it ain't about how hard ya hit. It's about how hard you can get hit and keep moving forward. How much you can take and keep moving forward. That's how winning is done!"

I want you to know in your darkest moments that there are people who love you and want to help you. You must know the truth that you are not alone. Sometimes we chose to be alone in the dark and wander around there for a while suffering because we think we have to.

The one choice you can control in your darkest moments is to invite others to come sit alongside you in the dark and be with you. They may not fix it. They may not know how to fix it. But just to have someone to be with you can make all the difference in your rising over it. We were made to connect to be together in all of life with both triumphs and tragedies. Don't go your failures alone. Open the window to your darkest night and let someone in. Someone you trust. Someone who cares. Someone who knows who you truly are.

We really do need each other in this life. Reciprocity. Give and take. Learn and be strong. Be vulnerable sometimes and strong other times. Don't be all or none.

One of my favorite movies was about the Boston Marathon. It was the famous hero who found himself later in a wheelchair after a bomb blew up and shattered his legs. There is a scene where he calls up his old girlfriend and tells her, "I really, really, really need you right now." In that moment I burst into tears realizing that I have never fully expressed myself to someone in that capacity. I might have danced around it hoping they could read my mind or timidly asked for what I needed.

But the truth is that no one can know what you need. They can't experience your truth's secret like you. It has to be revealed to be known. The depth of what your experiencing in this crazy mixed up game we call life is better shared. When you reveal it that is the opening to the most powerful moment of your life. I give you permission to need someone that bad.

The heroes in all our movies did and we root for them, don't we? So why can't you? Root for yourself. Are you blocking what you need somehow? Are you suffering it all alone? You don't have to. You can let someone come alongside you and just be there. It is a false belief to think we can't reveal negative things about ourselves, weaknesses and vulnerabilities.

You don't have to suffer every setback alone. You are allowed to need others as much as they need you. You are not perfect. You are allowed to not have all the answers, to risk, to connect with another human being at the highest level.

Think of it this way Iron Man had Pepper Potts, Superman had Lois Lane and Spiderman had Mary Jane Watson to rescue them, right? Even our bravest and buffest superheroes are going to need a little help to get them out of their crazy tight spots.
So do you my friend.

You know when you don't ask for help, you don't allow your partner, your family, your community to show up for you. You don't allow them the blessing of giving, or solving a problem with you. Life is going to have its seasons, turn, turn, turn... Superman runs out of Kryptonite and he is stuck until someone rescues him.

One of my favorite songs by Lauren Daigle is called Rescue. She sings about being there in the darkest night to rescue. Let someone in to rescue you. Don't leave yourself alone in your own life story and get stuck in the middle. The end is going to be amazing when you rewrite it in the middle. I believe connection is the strongest force on Earth to heal whatever you may be struggling with.

Below is an example of a Vulnerability wheel. Spin the spinner and make a choice to let someone come in.

Vulnerability Wheel

Self-Expression and Glory

"To go wrong in one's own way is better than to go right in someone else's."

Fyodor Dostoevsky

What does it mean to be fully self-expressed? This has been my biggest struggle most of my life. I found fear holding me back. Fear of not being enough. Resistance to who I truly am. Ever go to the gas station and the pump has air in it. The full power is blocked. That is how we are when we aren't letting all of us be expressed in life. We are clogged up and need a release so all of our channels are fully self-expressed. We need to squeeze the trigger all the way and let the power come out. Everything beautiful born deep inside ourselves released. We need to fully reveal ourselves and share our truth. It means we are confident and full of the expression of ourselves without holding anything back. We don't fear judgement, rejection, and criticism. We connect with our passions and purposes, our pizazz if you will. That's right. What sets you apart? We let ourselves be seen and known fully. What is the difference and contribution you can make? What might be blocking your self-expression?

I feel like the gluten allergy is like a clog of sorts. We have gluten inside our body that won't tolerate it and that blocks us up. So it is true of self-expression. In our lives we can live so much freer and fuller when we are totally self-expressed. What would this look like if you could tell anyone anything without holding back? How could your relationships, business, even love life become enhanced? I am talking about a better quality of life from being authentic and the best version of yourself; sharing all of yourself with those closest to you and also with the world.

Total self-expression is where our confidence shines. Some of us are creative souls that were born to do something completely different on this planet. You may be a play writer, a movie producer, a cartoon champion, a rap artist, a movie star or a dancer. Some discover their gift and receive accolades for it. Others hold onto their gift feeling different, afraid of being judged or being unsure of who they really are. You may be looking for a job and nothing fits you. You may be the brightest entrepreneur and it is time to craft the business plan. Step out and express your talents fully! Life comes to those who do every time.

Self-Expression Wheel

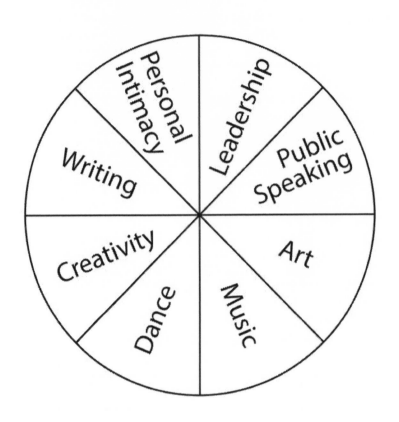

Stillness: The Soul's Food

"Be still and know that I am God."

We just don't have any in life. Freedom without agenda. I find myself sitting in the sun writing in my journal calming my soul. We absorb what is around us. Rushing, racing, chaos does not feed the soul. When did life get to be all about what we do, how we perform, how many emails we answer, how many tweets we tweet?

Our bodies need moments of stillness to heal. I don't think TV counts because the brain is engaged. We need reflection and quietness. A form of trust and surrender if you will. If I take this time out everything is not going to fall apart. I can just be. Just breathe. Inhale and exhale. Life was designed to be a serious of breaths where we inhale and exhale. A still small slow breath. Like a yogi on a mat flowing in and out rising and descending for the next pose.

I am after all my life. I am my breath. I am my body's health. I am not my circumstances, my finances, my stats. I am just me. There is value in my soul when I step aside. When I take a time out. There is value in my very being. If I am in touch with my worth I know I don't have to always perform and perform. When was the last time you let yourself just be?

Has life shown up for you in some areas over and over pulling you down or pushing you in? There is a stress syndrome that can grip your soul and it is toxic. It is wearing your energy thin. Stealing your

71

sleep. Pulling you away from your purpose. How do we show up for life differently? How do we cope with it all? How can we create a breakthrough in the middle of a breakdown?

Anxiety and thought patterns exist in a loop or chain. We tend to think the same thoughts in reaction to stress over and over. The best way to burst out of stress is to create something new. Let something powerful emerge out of you. If you can go to another coffee shop on the other side of town. Do It! Run in a new park. Try something completely different. Find a way to connect with your abilities to cope with the stress better. When we get outside of our normal routine we create a new loop. A new thought pattern. We show up better. More relaxed. Manifest change, growth, and resiliency. Buoyancy. The ability to bounce back and beyond. Get your step back after you feel beaten down and exhausted.

Stress Busters
1. Sunshine- Be in it!
2. Rest- Experience it.
3. Vitamins- get some
4. Exercise- make time
5. Vulnerability- let others in
6. Intimacy- create it
7. Connection- reach for it
8. Love- express it
9. Support- allow yourself to find it
10. Problem Solving- master it
11. Freedom- express it
12. Music- get more of it
13. Dance- let yourself move
14. Vacations- get away
15. Reciprocity- recognize you always have value

Digging out of Depression

"And something inside me just ... broke... that's the only way I could describe it."

Ranata Suzuki "

Did you know your gut can make you depressed? I experienced it many times. I wasn't myself. I felt tired, irritable and sad. I cried more easily. I was even anxious. It came on me suddenly and also had a heavy feeling accompanied by extreme indigestion. As I focused on what did I eat in the last 24 to 48 hours I realized I could fix the problem. When I ate a lot of sweets or heavy foods or had gluten reactions then it all plugged up my system and I wasn't myself.

This is a difficult space to navigate. To return yourself to ground zero and rise back again. I found when I eliminated the sugary foods I felt so much better. I had to be like a vigilante in my eating to restore the balance to my gut. Lots of probiotics and enzymes.

Realize when you are not feeling like yourself. I was even having extreme trouble sleeping from the food sensitivities waking up feeling exhausted. The intermittent fasting helped heal my digestion and get me back on track. There is a new app out there called LIFE Fasting Tracker that can help teach you how to use intermittent fasting.

In these times work gently with yourself and recognize when you are not feeling like you. Exercise helps. Social exercise even more so because it fulfills two things we need at one time; the need for connection and the dopamine release in the brain from exercise.

Dancing is a great form of social exercise. I don't care if you have two left feet and a third even. I went out on a day I was feeling particularly down. It was just a meet up with a band. I didn't know anyone. I learned I can't live with myself isolated and not functioning well. Push yourself when you are depressed to get out you will feel better.

My favorite moment is when I saw the shyest and sadly most overweight soul dancing to the song Gloria. I live where the Blues won the Stanley Cup and seeing that man come out of his shell on the dance floor brought such joy to my heart. We all deserve to get out, dance out, be out, and feel better. I will tell you a secret, no one is really looking at you on the dance floor. They are really looking at themselves. When you are free it liberates everyone around you. Even in your darkest moments you can experience freedom.

I was so happy I made myself get out and the music came alive to my body making the sad feelings bounce away with every beat. Exercise beats the blues every time!

Ultimately I began to learn that as I eliminated sugary foods which throw off the balance of the guts healthy bacteria I felt so much better. I had to eat less meat because my digestion was clogged.

If you are extremely busy try these life hacks.

1. Breakfast Date before work with an old friend
2. Coffee Date with anyone to catch up
3. Lunch Date with someone new
4. Movie Night with your spouse
5. One Day Off a Month no work
6. Skype Session with Loved Ones
7. Charity Event once a month
8. Volunteer an hour a week
9. Spiritual Retreat for a weekend

Gone Girl

"Your always one decision away from a totally different life."

Anonymous

This was a movie I never saw but it sounded intriguing. A woman who had perhaps disappeared and the mystery of her left unsolved. This is my story. Somewhere in the Gluten Free Freak story that same girl who started writing is gone. She is the gone girl. The mystery of her left behind and a new woman emerges braver, bolder, more confident. It is about time she came and has arrived. The grab and go girl when it came to her food is gone. The anxious striving soul as well has left the building. This girl on her journey to healing has had to examine every area of her life, not just what she puts into her gut. No more quick change artist will do for the life she is living.

I let this girl go. I was very afraid she had become my identity. But truly underneath it all this new woman was always there, just hiding behind what she thought she couldn't do. Who she thought she wasn't. Afraid to uncover and dish up to the world her authenticity. Her real deal.

You know what happens when you corner a raccoon? That's right, they are up for a fight. A big one! I will never forget my dad cornering a raccoon in our house. I was afraid for his life. That is what happens when we find ourselves facing adversity with our health, our energy and our vitality. We have to fight hard, the fight of our lifetime to come out the winner. You think that raccoon had losing on his mind when he bared his ugly teeth. Nope.

I know it is in you the fight, the will to deal with all this junk. Whether it is inflammation, celiac disease, joints that swell up or just wanting to be healthier. You can do it. You have got this. The fight of a lifetime is in you. Dig deep my friend. I have had to in order to overcome.

You know in one version of our lives we live a protected story. We take risks but only ones we are sure of the outcome. Our stories keep us in the safe place, the protected place in life. The place we can predict and control the outcome, even if it is small;
thinking we can't go any further. We assume we are not allowed to venture there. I don't know what it is on the other side of my comfort zone. I only know what it is right here on this side. Can I really be another person, a freer fully self-expressed person?

Can I perceive it? Can I see myself there? Coming forth. Emerging. Stepping out. Busting out. Breaking free. Daring and determined. Arriving just as I am. Showing up, being present, just carefree in the moment. All dressed up, on fire, just me ready for a lifetime of adventures and soul seeking fun. I finally got it. I am ready to burst out of my shell. Nobody is stopping me now. I hope you will join me on this crazy ride called life. Know that on the menu at the Venture Cafe is a thousand possibilities of how your life turns out. You pick and choose off the menu. I am having that one. This one serves my whole lifestyle of the powerful soul I am becoming.

Who do you want to be that you never get to be in life? Can you allow yourself that expression to emerge forth out of you? Try a new version of the menu of life. A sample of something you have never tasted before. Stop trying to control, be safe, and let the most authentic version of you show up. I promise you will never regret selecting the best you from the menu of life.

No Day but Today

"Forget regret or life is yours to miss, no other path, no other way. NO day but today."

Jonathan Larson

Did you know that we only have today? No day but today. My uncle had cancer and died on Christmas day and I remember my aunt and him had this motto, "No day but today." I finally got it that the things I am putting off manifesting in my life don't exist yet and never will till I take all my mojo and make them happen. We fool ourselves. We trick our minds into thinking the thing we seek like a gym workout will manifest in the near future. We tell ourselves I will get in shape later this week; when I clean the house, have more time, you know. When I am ready for it. It is really an excuse hanging over your life that you manifest to put off changing. Because change is so hard on the brain, the ego and the comfortable soul.

I keep looking at the future like I have all the time in the world and maybe some undefinable day down the road I will get started on my dreams. I am lying to myself as time marches on and she waits for no man or woman. She won't remind you later when you're older. Regret will show up in her place and settle in your soul with self-loathing and disgust.

This is your life talking to you. What do you really want? If you don't do it today there is really no other day. You have to push hard, want it bad, own up to how you have blocked it or been afraid to do it. All the things I currently have in my life are because of the choices I have made up to this point. If I don't have something it is because I haven't chosen it. I haven't put the pedal to the medal and gunned it.

Once you choose it is yours. It is in the intentionality of the will we create everything in life. Choose not to give up on the gluten free until you see the results you desire; the renewed energy, the better joints and the smaller waistline. The choice to live life at a different level is waiting for you. You level up with your choices. It all begins in the mind.

It finally struck me like a heavy chord that I don't have any more time to procrastinate, fool myself, and sign up later for the destiny. There is No Day but Today. I am completely in charge of all of it. This realization really came to me as I began to address my anxiety and cry out to God for him to deliver me where my own belief system kept me in the same cycle of life over and over again like Groundhogs Day.

I was postponing what I wanted thinking I possessed all the time in the world to create it all. Then when the brain fog lifted I got present to it. It is now or never. I am never going to be less afraid or more willing to make a hard choice someday. I have to plug into my ultimate source of power which is my faith in God and make the changes one by one.

I have to confront my fear of failure and missing the mark. We just think we have a lifetime to work things out. What goes around comes back around. If you don't deal with it today it will haunt you at some point. Why not today? Why not this very hour? What is on your list? The unfulfilled. The changes you need to make. Go to the doctor. Switch jobs. Start the business. Forgive a family member. Get real with yourself about what you really want. Don't play small. Don't live the defeatist over and over. Put this motto on your wall NO DAY BUT TODAY.

It will change everything! Stop holding yourself back in bondage by fear or pride, unwillingness to take full on responsibility for everything in your life. This day holds everything you need as you greet it in the early morning. As you send yourself off to bed make sure you manifest everything you desire.

Move with Your Body

"Refuse to let an old person move into your body."

Wayne Dyer

Move with your body baby! You have got to move more than ever. I know it is harder than ever with brain fog, exhaustion, anxiety and depression as they are all symptoms of a gluten allergy. I had them all. Plus food sensitivities that kept me up at night. As I moved more and was able to engage in core activities that engaged my breathing and used my diaphragm I began to heal faster. I could feel it. Revived energy and an interest in doing fun things.

The oxygen gets back flowing in your circulatory system and through your gut where the inflammation has settled. Don't settle on living a life with less than. You deserve more. More energy, vitality, more health, more capability to do what you love no matter your age. Moving with your body is unlike exercise. Because exercise comes up with resistance for a lot of folks.

Moving with your body is where you don't fight yourself. You move into the things you love to do and enable yourself the strength and energy to do them. I am not a gym rat. I do not ever want to be. But I sure do love to dance. I had muscle atrophy in one leg. I began to take back my life by going dancing even if I only lasted an hour. I was building my strength back inch by inch. You could even laugh at my clever plan. I would dance for an hour at public social swing or country dances.

Then I had to go sneak in the bathroom and stretch out my hip flexor. I had to leave early or arrive very late because I couldn't last the whole dance. I wore gym shoes with my pretty dress to support my back. Not ideal stats but the question is, "How bad do you want it?" How bad do you want to show up in the final hour of your life and live it full out and free? I don't care if your 65 or 75 get out on that dance floor and shake something while you still can.

If you want it bad you will do the crazy uncomfortable things whatever they may be. The first time I went dancing with all the muscle atrophy in my leg I didn't know if I could do it. The ladies might have stared at my big gym shoes with the dress, but most men sure didn't. They just looked at me as they swung me around on the dance floor as we danced to the crazy beat of a wild rock band. I had a blast and got over my story about how I can't dance with a bum leg.

Whatever you find to do in the universe, do it! I saw a woman with two robotic legs give a speech while only standing on one of them. Now that is commitment! Whatever you love don't let some achy joints stop you. Get out there and do it anyway! When you take the energy to inspire yourself and show up for yourself you wind up inspiring your whole world as they watch.

Golf, garden, walk the dog, even shopping is moving. I once shopped with two seventy year old ladies all day and had to stop to rest. They moved to over 6 stores. Yes shopping is exercise. Flea marketing. Trying on clothes. Antique shopping. Whatever your pleasure do it! Put the hustle back in your step. Hunting, fishing, climbing stairs, Pilates, isometrics, yoga are all moving.

Some days I was so tired I just headed to the gym and punched a boxing bag for 10 min. That is the best 10 min of the week. Gets the heart rate up and made me feel great. I discovered backwards water walking which unlocked my very tight hip flexors. And my favorite activity in the summer was going to the lazy river at the kiddie pool and walking against the current. Just have fun and move. Chase the kids, the dog, the hot guy or gal around the house. You know what I mean. It extends the quality of our lives and it helps the body to heal when we have inflammation. Don't try to move like the people at the gym. Don't put false expectations on yourself. You're not competing against them. Only yourself. Every day get better at stepping into the flow of the life you want to create.

On my worst days when my Sacroiliac joint flared up my moving consisted of 10 min of stretching before bed to get the pain out of my joints. Our bodies were made to move. The word exercise comes with so much resistance. Think of moving as a reward. You get to move. You have legs. You are not on your death bed. Even grabbing some resistance bands for ten minutes feels great.

I found a killer upper body to help my posture so I don't get a neck ache. That is moving with your body. Your making you feel better, more productive and stronger. Track and trend your movements if you can to see progress. My arms are weak. So today I do 3 sets of 10 with the bands and tomorrow I aim for 3 sets of 12. Write it down. If you want a stronger body go after it!

Carpe Diem! Seize the day! I know there will be those days you don't feel like it but I guarantee you that this gluten free freak went from feeling down and out to amazing with just moving her body. There are the days the freaking allergies keep me down but I don't let those days last. Don't allow yourself to be overcome. You are an overcomer!

There is always a way while we are on this earth to move our bodies. I even have exercises I do in bed to strengthen my core. Clam shells and some dead bugs, an amazing exercise you can google. One of my favorite all time Instagram people is docjenfit. She came up with an entire system of how to overcome limitations in the body. She has videos on Instagram for each area of the body and she is a physical therapist. She inspired me so much in stretching to believe I could increase my range of motion. Even after life has knocked you down, get back up.

Remember Jack Lelane from the 1960's he was pushing fit on the TV. At the age of 90 he could still do 90 pushups. I have met 90 years old who go bowling and serve in soup kitchens. It is a paradigm shift that as we age we get worse. You get whatever your mindset tells you that you get. Don't like what has been happening to your body. Manifest something else. Expect abundant energy. Expect to be rowdy and rambunctious in your 50's, 60's and 70's. Expect more, create more and you will have more.

If you're not feeling it make a commitment to yourself that you will do you at the highest level in this life you can. Show up for yourself. Push yourself. Stretch yourself. The end result is worth the work. Finish the race, run the marathon of taking your health to the next level just by showing up for yourself. You deserve the best life after all. You only get one go at it. There is no do over. Make it a rich and full one. The best life. One day an older you will thank you for the sacrifices you made along the way. For the grit and the grind it took to overcome just to be free to move your body when it hurt, when you didn't feel like it and when it seemed like the struggle overcame you more than the reward. The quality of life is your quest.

First Day of the Rest of Your Life

What do you want to wake up to? What don't you want on your plate anymore? Let's clear the plate today. Literally make a list. I don't want anymore... Drama, joint pain, stress, weight gain, depression, brain fog, sleeplessness, low energy... you name it.

_____

_____

_____

_____

_____

_____

_____

_____

I will add to my plate more_____. (Joy, freedom, love, self-care, connection, intimacy, fun, laughter, rest, creative time, solitude, magic, abundance)

No Day but Today

Today I am giving up holding onto _____.

And I am letting go of it all. NO longer will my days be marked by a struggle with _____.

I am committing to myself 110 % to take charge of the following outcomes.

1. Mindset
2. Moving with my body
3. Spiritual growth
4. Connection
5. Vulnerability
6. Creating my own life map.

What do you want your health to do for you? Why should you move more? What is your ultimate why? Wake up pain free. Wake up celebrating aging. Wake up able to do what you love which includes more of the following:

I want a body that can _____. (Tango dance, fish, hunt, rock climb, stretch, do areal yoga)

I want the energy to _____ (play with my grandkids, travel, speak, start a business)

As I age my top priority is to _____ (not lose my muscle mass, flexibility, strength or cardio endurance)

I am committed to strong self-care by taking the following action _____ (plan my meals, high intensity workouts, gratitude before bed, accountability partner for my goals)

My passion list: (The things I love to do. Important to remember on my darkest days)

_____

_____

_____

_____

_____

_____

My ultimate reasons:

_____

_____

_____

_____

_____

_____

Legacy I want to create for those nearest and dearest to me:

I most want to be remembered for:

_____

_____

_____

_____

_____

_____

_____

_____

My legacy I commit to creating after me begins with the first step of:

_____

_____

_____

_____

_____

_____

_____

_____

_____

My destiny statement (The mission you have on this earth. To use
your talents for a higher purpose to serve others in some way shape
or form)

_____

_____

_____

_____

_____

_____

_____

_____

_____

My Life Map

Moving with Your Body

When I am old, very old, I still want to be able to

_____.

Bowl, dance, and swim you name it! Met a 90 year old who went bowling 3 times a week!

I commit to moving my body 150 min a week. 30 min 5 times a week or more. I will keep a journal of my fav exercises.

What is my dream body? What do my muscles look like? What is my BMI and percentage of body fat?

_____.

What do I want to be able to do? How will I map it out to get there step by step?

_____

_____

_____

_____

_____

_____

_____

_____

_____

Strength; Weight, Resistance, Isometrics, Machines and Yoga

Flexibility; Stretching Yoga, Pilates

Fun Movement; Dance, Gardening, Hiking, Biking, Swimming, Dancing, Tennis, Golf

Motivation for Exercise:

_____

Fit into skinny jeans, go on a rock climbing trip, and enter a dance competition.

Music to motivate me to work out: Get the playlist on!!

Podcasts to work out to

_____

My fav Audible List of books to keep me going_____

Weekly reward. If I keep my end of the bargain. On the weekend I get to indulge in:

_____
_____
_____
_____
_____

Self-Expression Map

In what areas of my life is my self-expression blocked? Public speaking, interpersonal communication, being a leader at work, sharing my ideas to my boss, asking for the money I deserve, expressing myself creatively through writing, poetry or art, dance.

What does my life look life with unlimited full on self-expression?

Public Speaking freely going anywhere. Speaking to a crowd of 100, 1000, 10.000

Conversations with my Spouse, Boss, those in my inner circle,

I will commit to becoming more fully self-expressed by trying the following out of my comfort zone.

_____
_____
_____
_____
_____
_____

Connection: Social Circles

I want to expand my social circles for my business, fun, work, etc. How will I become more connected to my community?

_____

_____

_____

_____

I can volunteer one hour a week doing...

_____

I can attend a new meet up, club, organization or event on

_____

I can create more powerful social circles by going to the following events in my city

_____

_____

_____

_____

_____

_____

_____

_____

_____

Vulnerability

I need the people closest to me to know that I need:

_____

_____

_____

_____

_____

_____

_____

I will begin to express what I truly need by asking for help in the area of:

_____

_____

_____

_____

_____

_____

_____

_____

In case you have been diagnosed with Celiac disease the following two pages are for you to copy and use to send out if you want to let family and friends know before you come to visit and aren't sure how to put it into words. I cried when I wrote mine, but life is a joyful and blissful event when we live it out fully. Be blessed beloved. You are God's most precious child and He loves you so much beyond measure.

Dear Family and Friends,

I was diagnosed with celiac disease. I wanted to write this letter to explain to you about it so when I come to your house for dinner or the holidays you understand why I can't eat all your food and what you can do to help me out. Celiac disease is a severe allergic reaction to wheat that damages the intestines. The villa in my intestine cannot absorb nutrients. I must be on a very strict diet the rest of my life in order to heal my colon.

If I am not I could die from malnutrition. My body responds to gluten as an invader and my autoimmune system attacks my own body when I eat it. I also am one of the lucky souls who happen to break out in a severe gluten rash when I eat any gluten. The rash is very aggressive and takes drugs to overcome so I need to avoid being cross contaminated at all costs. I also am allergic to milk and all forms of dairy now.

The good news is that there are all kinds of gluten free flours, certified gluten free restaurants and certified gluten free frozen prepared foods. I can go to the grocery store with you when I arrive and pick out my own gluten free snacks, food or bread. I cannot have anything that has been cooked next to flour because of the danger of cross contamination. I can eat all meat, vegetables and fresh produce.

There are gluten free bakeries or we can make something together from scratch for dessert that is gluten free. I plan on living a long and healthy life and know together we can do this. Thanks for your understanding and support. Life is a precious gift. It is not really all about the food, but what we can create in the kitchen and with our lives together. There is No Day but Today we are promised and I am so grateful for each and every one of you who makes my life richer and more sweet.

My Lifelong Commitment to Myself

I hereby pledge and commit to myself that I will not grab and go food on the run. I will plan and prepare my meals. I will not forget to think of all the details when I travel, have crazy long days or any days for that matter. Everything that goes into my mouth makes up my health, well-being and longevity. I matter and I am worth the time I need to commit to all the planning and preparation. I plan to live the longest life possible and I will not be taken out by anything called disease or with the name Celiac. I am signing this today to commit to myself and my own self-care in love of my life and how precious it is to give myself the best possible chances in life.

_____

The End or Just the Beginning

The creative soul in me knows that what we manifest every day, every moment, every choice creates the end of our story. If we don't like it at any point we must simply forgive ourselves and make another choice. The end is just the beginning of limitless possibilities.

Well today I walked around the track and that was a moment of victory for me! I remember the beginning of my story when I had trouble just plain walking due to joint inflammation. In the middle of the story I marveled when I could walk around the gym four times, but honestly I never would have seen the track in my future.

That's it we can't see the glory till we take the first few initial steps out of our pain. Know my friend that there is an end goal for you so glorious in your future. You can become unstoppable, yes you can! The journey of a thousand miles begins with one tiny step. I am a Mindset Coach and I do private coaching for individuals. Please reach out to me if you are interested in coaching at meedermarianne@gmail.com.